W9-BHK-427

Soup
MANIA ®

Macmillan Canada

Toronto

Soup Mania®

Copyright © 1998

Canadian Cataloguing in Publication Data

Main entry under title:
Soup mania

ISBN 0-7715-7586-6

1. Soups.

TX757.S67 1998   641.8'13   C98-931450-2

1 2 3 4 5 TRI 02 01 00 99 98

This book is available at special discounts for bulk purchases by your
group or organization for sales promotions, premiums, fundraising and
seminars. For details, contact: Macmillan Canada, Special Sales Department,
29 Birch Avenue, Toronto, ON M4V 1E2. Tel: 416-963-8830.

Cover photo: Hal Roth

Macmillan Canada
A Division of Canada Publishing Corporation
Toronto, Ontario, Canada

Printed in Canada

CONTENTS

TIPS ON MAKING SOUPS

A SOUP made with home-made stock is always going to be the best soup you could feed your family and friends. That being said, some of you don't have the time, the energy or the desire to make stock from scratch, and if that's the case, then don't. Where you see that a recipe calls for stock, you can use canned, powdered, paste or cubes. Just follow the directions on the container and substitute equal amounts.

Have fun with garnishes. Use your imagination: make coloured swirls with sour cream, pesto or even jam. (Just remember that a liquid garnish works best if it's a little heavier than the soup—that way, it stays in place.) Sprinkles of herbs, slivers of red pepper or even vegetable or toast shapes made with cookie cutters can turn your soup presentation into a work of art.

The thickness and texture of your finished product will vary depending on the size, freshness and starch content of the vegetables you use. So, if you finish making the soup and it's too thick, just add more of whatever type of liquid—stock, water or juice—you used. If it's too thin, let it cook on top of the stove until some of the liquid reduces, or add one or more teaspoons of potato flour until it is the thickness you want. Potato flour is better than wheat flour for last-minute thickening because it won't make your broth lumpy and it doesn't have the same floury taste.

Garnishes

Cheese Twisties

These delicious Twisties are simple to make and will impress any dinner guest. They'll keep at room temperature for several days.

> 1 package frozen unbaked puff pastry
> ½ lb cheddar cheese, grated

Thaw pastry and remove from box.

Lay pastry out flat and sprinkle with cheese.

Cut into 1-inch strips and twist.

Refrigerate for 20 minutes.

Bake according to the directions on the package.

Yields 20.

Garlic Croutons

These go with every kind of soup and will keep at room temperature indefinitely.

1 French stick
5 cloves garlic
3 tbsp dried thyme
1 tsp salt
½ cup olive oil

Preheat oven to 350°F.

Slice French stick into 1-inch-thick pieces.

Purée remaining ingredients in food processor.

Brush garlic oil onto bread.

Bake on baking tray for 5 minutes.

Turn croutons over and bake for 5 more minutes or until golden.

Yields 25.

Fancy Bread

You can have a lot of fun with these. Try using seasonal cookie cutters—you can serve little festive characters in your holiday soup!

> ½ lb butter, soft
> 2 tsp garlic powder
> 2 tsp onion powder
> 1 tsp salt
> 1 loaf of your favourite bread, sliced

Preheat oven to 350°F.

Mix butter with spices and salt.

Spread butter mixture on bread slices.

Using cookie cutters, cut shapes out of bread.

Bake on baking tray for 5 minutes on each side or until toasted.

Yields 20.

Meatballs

Great to serve in soups, stews and pastas.

> 1 medium onion
> 1 rib celery
> 1-½ lb ground beef or veal
> 5 tbsp minced garlic
> 2 large eggs
> 1 cup bread crumbs
> ½ tbsp salt
> ¼ tsp black pepper

Preheat oven to 350°F.

Mince onion and celery in the food processor.

Combine with remaining ingredients in a medium bowl and mix well by hand.

Form into 1-inch balls. Keep hands moist with cold water to prevent sticking.

Bake on baking tray for 20 minutes or until meat is no longer pink inside.

Yields 20.

Potato Dumplings

These tasty tidbits are worth the time and trouble.

> 2 medium potatoes
> 1 tsp onion powder
> 1 tbsp parsley flakes
> 5 tbsp flour
> ¼ tsp salt
> Pinch white pepper
> Pinch nutmeg
> 2 egg yolks

Preheat oven to 350°F.

Bake potatoes for 1 hour or until they yield easily when squeezed.

Peel and mash potatoes while they are still warm.

Combine dry ingredients and mix with potato.

Stir in egg yolks until smooth.

Roll the dough into a log about ½ inch thick. Slice into 1-inch pieces, roll into balls and place on baking tray.

Cover and refrigerate for 15 minutes.

Poach in 3 quarts of salted, simmering water, stock or soup for 10 minutes.

Yields 30.

Buttermilk Dumplings

Old-fashioned goodness to add to your soups.

> 1-½ cups flour
> 1 tbsp baking powder
> ½ tsp salt
> 1 tbsp parsley flakes
> 2 tbsp cold butter
> 1 large egg
> ½ cup buttermilk

Mix together dry ingredients.

Chop butter into small pieces. Using your hands, rub butter into flour mixture.

Beat egg and mix with buttermilk.

Stir liquid ingredients into flour mixture until the dough forms a ball.

Lightly flour your hands, roll dough into balls and place on baking tray.

Cover and refrigerate for 15 minutes.

Poach in 3 quarts of salted, simmering water, stock or soup for 10 minutes.

Yields 30.

Stocks

Chicken Stock

Wisdom has it that a soup is only as good as the stock you cook into it. Most people think a good stock is hard to make—messy and time consuming—but that just isn't true. This stock is easy as pie and worth the trouble just for the wonderful aroma that will fill your kitchen while it simmers.

> 1 rib celery
> 2 medium onions
> 2 medium carrots
> 4 lb chicken bones (backs are great for stock)
> 2 bay leaves

Remove any leaves from the celery. You don't even have to peel the vegetables: just quarter them and throw them in, skins and all.

Put everything into your soup pot and cover it with cold water.

Bring it to a boil and reduce the heat; let it simmer for 3–4 hours.

As it cooks, keep adding cold water to cover bones and skim any scum that forms on top.

Remove from heat, strain and let cool.

This delicious stock will keep in your fridge for 4 days or your freezer for 4 weeks.

Beef Stock

This one is harder and takes longer than the chicken stock. Still, be brave and give it a try!

> 5 lb beef bones (knuckles or shoulders work well)
> 2 medium onions
> 2 medium carrots
> 2 ribs celery
> 2 tbsp tomato paste

Preheat oven to 400°F.

Arrange bones on a baking tray and roast for about 2 hours, turning occasionally. You want them browned but not burned.

Don't bother to peel the vegetables; just wash and quarter them. Remove any leaves from the celery. Add vegetables to baking tray for the last 20 minutes. Take vegetables and bones from the oven and place in your soup pot. Add a little water to the tray and scrape any brown bits from the bottom into the pot.

Add cold water to the pot to cover contents and bring to boil.

Reduce heat, add tomato paste and simmer for 4–5 hours.

As the stock is cooking, keep adding cold water to cover bones and skim any scum that forms.

Remove from heat, strain and let cool.

This stock will keep in your fridge for 4 days or your freezer for 4 weeks.

Vegetable Stock

Vegetarians can use this stock to add richness to many of our soups. An even quicker Chinese vegetable stock is made by covering 1 pound of bean sprouts with cold water, bringing it to a boil, then simmering for 15 minutes and straining.

> 1 medium onion
> 2 medium carrots
> 2 ribs celery
> ¼ head green cabbage
> 1 bay leaf
> 1 bunch parsley (optional)

Peel and chop the vegetables into large pieces.

Add all ingredients to soup pot.

Cover with cold water and bring to a boil.

Reduce heat and simmer for 45 minutes.

Remove from heat, strain and let cool.

This stock will keep in the fridge for 3 days or the freezer for 4 weeks.

Fish Stock

The easiest and fastest stock of them all—you can go from scratch to chowder in under an hour.

> 2 lb bones of any white-fleshed fish
> 1 medium onion
> 2 medium carrots
> 1 leek (white part only)
> 1 bunch parsley

Put all ingredients into soup pot and cover with cold water.

Bring to boil. Reduce and let simmer for 30 minutes.

Skim off any scum that comes to the surface during cooking.

Remove from heat, strain and let cool.

Stock will keep in the fridge for 2 days or the freezer for 4 weeks.

Soups

*All the recipes in the book are designed
to serve 6 hearty portions.*

Chicken Noodle Soup

Everyone's favourite. No cook's recipe file is complete without this classic.

> 1 medium onion, diced
> 2 ribs celery, diced
> 3 medium carrots, diced
> 3 boneless skinless chicken breasts, cubed
> 3 tbsp butter
> 7 cups chicken stock
> 2 cups egg noodles
> 3 tbsp lemon juice
> 3 tbsp chopped fresh parsley

Cook onion, celery, carrot and chicken in butter over medium heat until onion is soft.

Add stock and bring to boil.

Reduce heat and simmer for 20 minutes.

Bring back to boil and add noodles, lemon juice and parsley and cook for 5 minutes or until noodles are soft.

Cock-a-Leekie

Prunes make this rendition of a standard a little exotic.

> 5 leeks (white parts only), sliced
> 3 boneless skinless chicken breasts, cubed
> 3 tbsp butter
> 6 cups chicken stock
> 1 bay leaf
> 6 oz pitted prunes, chopped
> Salt and black pepper

Cook the leeks and the chicken in butter until the leeks are soft.

Add the stock and bay leaf and bring to boil.

Reduce heat to simmer and add prunes.

Let simmer for 20 minutes.

Discard bay leaf and add salt and pepper to taste.

After-the-Roast Soup

The best way to use leftovers from any poultry roast—turkey,
chicken or duck—is to make a wonderful soup the next day.
Potato or Buttermilk Dumplings (see pages 6 and 7) would
suit this soup to a T.

> Carcass of roasted poultry
> 1 bay leaf
> 4 medium carrots, chopped
> 2 medium onions, chopped
> 2 tbsp oil
> 2 cups leftover roasted vegetables, chopped
> 1 cup frozen peas
> 1 tbsp tomato paste
> 1 tbsp Worcestershire sauce
> 3 cups leftover poultry pieces, chopped

Remove the large pieces of meat from the carcass but leave on smaller bits like wings. Remove any fat or skin.

Break the bones up a little and put in soup pot. Cover with cold water and bring to boil.

Reduce heat and simmer for 2 hours with bay leaf, one-quarter of the carrots and half the onion. Strain and skim off any fat.

In another soup pot, cook remaining carrots and onions in oil until soft.

Add the stock you just prepared, any defatted pan juices or gravy from the roast, roasted vegetables, peas, tomato paste and Worcestershire.

Bring to a boil and reduce heat. Add leftover poultry.

Discard bay leaf and add salt and pepper to taste.

One-Eyed Jack Soup

This basic soup makes a great refresher to serve during an afternoon card game.

6 cups chicken stock
1 tbsp lemon juice
½ tsp salt
6 large eggs
3 green onions, chopped
6 tbsp grated Parmesan cheese
6 Garlic Croutons (see page 3)

Bring stock to a boil. Add lemon juice and salt.

Poach eggs in stock for approx. 3 minutes or until done.

Add green onions and cheese.

Each bowl should be served with one egg sitting on one crouton.

Corny Chicken Soup

Here's a soup fit to tame a hungry mob.

1 (3 lb) chicken
1 medium onion, chopped
1 bay leaf
1 tsp dried thyme
2-½ cups frozen corn
¼ cup barley

Cut chicken into 8 pieces and put in soup pot.

Cover with cold water and add onions, bay leaf and thyme.

Poach for 40 minutes, topping with cold water, and skim any scum that forms. Remove chicken from pot.

Bring soup to a boil and add corn and barley.

Reduce heat and simmer for 30 minutes.

Remove chicken meat from bone and chop. Return to soup.

Discard bay leaf.

Bat and Ball Soup

Any little athletes in the house will love this sporty number.

> 1 medium onion, diced
> 2 medium carrots, diced
> 2 ribs celery, diced
> 6 chicken drumsticks, skin removed
> 3 tbsp cooking oil
> 7 cups chicken stock
> Salt and black pepper
> 30 Potato Dumplings (see page 6)

Brown vegetables and drumsticks in oil.

Add stock and bring to boil.

Reduce heat and simmer for 30 minutes.

Add salt and pepper to taste.

Add dumplings and poach for 10 minutes.

Chicken Soup with Buttermilk Dumplings

Straight from Grandma's recipe box to your kitchen.

> 1 medium onion
> 2 medium carrots
> 2 ribs celery
> 2 medium parsnips
> 1 white turnip
> 3 boneless skinless chicken breasts
> 3 tbsp butter
> 7 cups chicken stock
> 1 bay leaf
> Salt and black pepper
> 18 Buttermilk Dumplings (see page 7)

Cube the vegetables and chicken breasts.

Brown in butter.

Add stock and bay leaf and bring to boil.

Reduce heat and simmer for 30 minutes.

Discard bay leaf and add salt and pepper to taste.

Poach dumplings in soup for 10 minutes.

Cream of Chicken Soup

This soup looks great with brightly coloured garnishes like thin slices of red and green pepper, or a couple of sprigs of chives.

1 medium onion, diced
5 tbsp butter
5 tbsp flour
3 cups chicken stock, cold
3 boneless skinless chicken breasts, cubed
2 ribs celery, diced
1 green pepper, seeded and diced
1 bay leaf
1 whole clove
2 cups 35 percent cream
1 cup white wine
Pinch nutmeg
Salt and black pepper

Cook onions in butter until soft.

Add flour and cook, stirring for 3–4 minutes.

Gradually add stock, stirring, and bring to boil.

Add wine, chicken, vegetables, bay leaf and clove.

Reduce heat and simmer for 20 minutes.

Stir in cream and nutmeg and simmer for 5-10 minutes.

Discard bay leaf and clove and add salt and pepper to taste.

Lamb Sausage and Rice Soup

A very popular dish in Mennonite country, where traditional farming methods produce fabulous lamb.

> 1 medium onion, diced
> 2 tsp minced garlic
> 1 lb lamb sausage, sliced
> 1 cup parboiled rice
> 7 cups beef or lamb stock
> 1 tbsp tomato paste
> Salt and black pepper

Brown onions, garlic and sausage over medium-high heat.

Stir in rice. Cook for 3 minutes.

Add stock and tomato paste and bring to boil.

Reduce heat and simmer for 25 minutes.

Add salt and pepper to taste.

Bill's Beef Barley Soup

This robust soup is ideal to warm winter-weary spirits.

> 1 lb stewing beef
> 1 medium onion, diced
> 1 medium carrot, diced
> 1 rib celery, diced
> 2 tsp minced garlic
> 2 tbsp cooking oil
> 6 cups beef stock
> ⅓ cup barley
> 1 bay leaf
> Salt and black pepper

Cut beef into 1-inch cubes.

Brown beef, onion, carrot, celery and garlic in oil.

Add beef stock, barley and bay leaf.

Bring to boil.

Reduce heat and let simmer for 1-½ hours.

Discard bay leaf and add salt and pepper to taste.

Onion Soup

We've simplified this traditional treat to make it easy to cook at home.

> 10 medium red onions (about 3 lb), sliced
> ¼ lb butter
> 5 cups beef stock
> 1 cup sweet sherry
> 1 bay leaf
> 2 tsp minced garlic
> 6 slices thick-cut bread
> 6 slices mozzarella cheese

Brown onions in butter.

Add stock, sherry, bay leaf and garlic and bring to boil.

Reduce heat and let simmer for 30 minutes.

Discard bay leaf.

Preheat broiler.

Toast bread and use a soup bowl to cut rounds that will fit exactly into your bowls.

Top the cut toasts with mozzarella cheese and broil them on a baking tray until the cheese melts.

Serve the toasts on top of your soup for a smart finishing touch.

Beef and Mushroom Soup

Cloudy skies and rainy days call for this perfect comfort food.

> 1 lb stewing beef
> ¾ lb mushrooms
> 1 medium carrot, diced
> 1 medium onion, diced
> 2 tbsp minced garlic
> 3 tbsp butter
> ½ cup brandy
> 5 cups beef stock
> 2 tbsp Worcestershire sauce
> Salt and black pepper

Cut beef into 1-inch cubes and slice mushrooms.

Brown beef, carrot, onion and garlic in butter.

Add mushrooms and brandy and cook for 5 minutes.

Add stock and Worcestershire and bring to a boil.

Reduce heat and let simmer for 1 hour.

Add salt and pepper to taste.

Chili Soup in a Bread Bowl

Encourage your guests to eat the bowl.

> ½ lb ground beef
> 1 medium onion, diced
> 1 tbsp minced garlic
> 1 chili pepper (optional)
> 2 cans (19 oz each) red kidney beans, undrained
> 2 cans (28 oz each) plum tomatoes, undrained
>   and tomatoes squished
> 3 cups chicken stock or water
> 6 large pumpernickel or crusty buns
> 1 cup grated cheddar cheese

Brown ground beef, onion, garlic and chili pepper, if using. Drain off any excess fat.

Rinse and drain kidney beans and add with tomatoes and stock.

Bring to boil. Reduce heat and let simmer for 20 minutes.

To make bread bowls, cut a slice off the top of each bun.

Scoop out the inside, leaving a bowl shape about ¼ inch thick.

You can serve the bowls as is or toast them in the oven for 10 minutes.

Pour soup in bowl and sprinkle with cheddar cheese.

Gumbo Mumbo Jumbo

A taste of Southern hospitality in a bowl.

3 strips bacon, chopped
1 medium onion, diced
2 tsp minced garlic
1 chili pepper (optional)
1 tbsp butter
½ lb sausage
2 boneless skinless chicken breasts
1 cup cubed okra
1 can (5 oz) clams, drained
1 can (28 oz) plum tomatoes, undrained
   and tomatoes squished
½ cup rice
5 cups chicken stock
1 bay leaf

Cook bacon, onions, garlic and chili pepper, if using, in butter until soft.

Cube sausage and chicken. Add to pot along with okra and brown.

Add remaining ingredients and bring to boil.

Reduce heat and let simmer for 30–40 minutes.

Discard bay leaf.

Hungarian Beef Pot

Serve this soup with a big dollop of sour cream—just like paprikash!

> 1-½ lb stewing beef
> ½ medium onion, diced
> 2 tsp minced garlic
> 2 tbsp cooking oil
> 1 chili pepper (optional)
> 2 tbsp paprika
> ½ tsp salt
> ½ tsp caraway seeds
> 2 medium potatoes, peeled and cubed
> 1 green pepper, seeded and diced
> 5 cups beef stock or water
> 1 cup 35 percent cream
> Salt and black pepper

Cut beef into 1-inch cubes.

Brown beef, onion and garlic in oil.

Add chili pepper, if using, paprika, salt, caraway seeds, potatoes and green pepper and stir.

Add stock and bring to boil. Reduce heat and simmer for 1 hour.

Add cream and simmer for 5 minutes.

Add salt and pepper to taste.

That's a Spicy Meatball

Kids will love eating this soup, which is full of fun.

> 1 medium red onion
> 1 medium carrot
> 1 medium parsnip
> 2 tsp minced garlic
> 1 tbsp olive oil
> 4 cups beef stock
> 1 can (28 oz) plum tomatoes, undrained
>   and tomatoes squished
> 1 chili pepper (optional)
> 30 Meatballs (see page 5)
> 3 tbsp grated Parmesan cheese

Dice vegetables.

Cook vegetables and garlic in oil over medium heat for 5 minutes.

Add stock, tomatoes and chili pepper, if using, and bring to boil.

Reduce heat and simmer for 10 minutes.

Add cooked meatballs and simmer for 10 more minutes.

Serve with Parmesan cheese.

Heavenly Hash

Here's a salute to Fabulous Fifties cuisine.

>1 medium onion
>1 red pepper, seeded
>1 green pepper, seeded
>1 medium potato, peeled
>2 tbsp flour
>2-½ tbsp butter
>½ lb cooked ham, cubed
>½ lb corned beef, cubed
>½ lb cooked roast beef, cubed
>5 cups beef stock, cold

Chop vegetables.

Cook vegetables and flour in butter over medium heat for 5 minutes.

Stir in meat. Gradually add stock, stirring, and bring to boil.

Reduce heat and simmer for 20 minutes.

Everything-in-the-Fridge Soup

A bit of this and a bit of that combine to make this eclectic soup.

1 medium onion, sliced
1 medium parsnip, peeled and diced
1 rib celery, diced
3 tbsp butter
1 lb cooked ham, roast beef or chicken, cubed
6 cups chicken stock
½ cup frozen corn
½ cup frozen peas
½ cup frozen carrots
1 cup broccoli florets

Cook onions, parsnip and celery in butter until soft.

Stir in meat.

Add stock and bring to a boil.

Reduce and let simmer for 10 minutes.

Add frozen vegetables and bring back to boil.

Add broccoli and reduce heat.

Simmer for 5 minutes and serve.

Lamb Soup with Buttermilk Dumplings

A hard day and a hungry heart call for this soothing soup.

> 1-½ lb boneless lamb shoulder
> 1 medium onion
> 1 medium carrot
> 1 rib celery
> ½ lb mushrooms
> 2 tsp minced garlic
> 3 tbsp butter
> 7 cups beef stock
> 2 tbsp tomato paste
> 1 bay leaf
> Salt and black pepper
> 30 Buttermilk Dumplings (see page 7)

Clean fat from lamb and cut into 1-inch cubes.

Peel and cube onion, carrot and celery.

Slice mushrooms.

Brown lamb, vegetables and garlic in butter.

Add stock, tomato paste and bay leaf. Bring to boil.

Reduce heat and simmer for 1 hour.

Discard bay leaf and add salt and pepper to taste.

Poach dumplings in soup for 10 minutes.

Beef Soup with Potato Dumplings

A wonderful stick-to-your-ribs classic.

1 medium onion
1 medium carrot
1 medium parsnip
1 white turnip
1-½ lb stewing beef
2 tbsp butter
1 tbsp tomato paste
1 tbsp prepared mustard
1 bay leaf
7 cups beef stock
Salt and black pepper
30 Potato Dumplings (see page 6)

Peel and cube vegetables.

Cut beef into 1-inch cubes.

Brown beef and vegetables in butter.

Stir in tomato paste, mustard and bay leaf.

Add stock and bring to boil.

Reduce heat and simmer for 1 hour.

Discard bay leaf and add salt and pepper to taste.

Poach dumplings in soup for 10 minutes.

Beef and Bow-Tie Soup

Bow-tie pasta dresses up this favourite.

> 1 lb stewing beef
> 1 tbsp Italian seasoning
> 2 tbsp cooking oil
> 1 bay leaf
> 1 can (28 oz) plum tomatoes, undrained
>   and tomatoes squished
> 8 cups beef stock
> 2 cups frozen mixed vegetables
> 1 cup bow-tie pasta
> Salt and black pepper

Cut beef into 1-inch cubes.

Brown beef in Italian seasoning and oil.

Add bay leaf, tomatoes and stock and bring to boil.

Reduce heat and simmer for 1 hour.

Add frozen vegetables and return to boil.

Add pasta and cook for about 12 minutes or follow directions on package.

Discard bay leaf and add salt and pepper to taste.

Serve with Garlic Croutons (see page 3) or Fancy Bread (see page 4).

Pizza Pie Soup

This zany recipe will have your kids calling for more.

> 1 medium onion
> ½ lb cooked ham
> 1 lb pepperoni
> ½ lb mushrooms
> 2 tsp minced garlic
> 1 tsp Italian seasoning
> 3 tbsp cooking oil
> 1 can (28 oz) plum tomatoes, undrained
> and tomatoes squished
> 5 cups chicken stock
> 1 bay leaf
> Salt and black pepper
> 1 cup grated mozzarella cheese

Cut onion, ham and pepperoni into 1-inch cubes.

Slice mushrooms.

Brown first six ingredients in oil.

Add tomatoes, stock and bay leaf and bring to boil.

Reduce heat and simmer for 20 minutes.

Discard bay leaf and add salt and pepper to taste.

Top with mozzarella cheese and serve with Cheese Twisties (see page 2).

Country Cabbage Soup

A taste of pastoral heaven.

> 2 medium onions, sliced
> 1 medium carrot, diced
> 3 ribs celery, diced
> 2 tbsp cooking oil
> ½ head green cabbage
> ½ lb cooked roast beef
> ¾ lb sausages
> 6 cups beef stock
> 2 tsp dried thyme

Cook onions, carrot and celery in oil over medium heat for 5 minutes.

Slice cabbage and stir into vegetables.

Cube beef and sausage and add to vegetables.

Add stock and thyme and bring to boil.

Reduce heat and simmer for 45 minutes.

Shrimp Bisque

We've taken the difficulty out of making this seafarer's delight.

1 medium onion
2 medium carrots
2 ribs celery
1 lb frozen peeled uncooked shrimp
5 tbsp butter
5 tbsp flour
1 cup white wine
4 cups fish stock or water
1 bay leaf
2 tsp tomato paste
2 cups 35 percent cream

Dice onion, carrots and celery.

Cook shrimp and vegetables in butter over medium heat
for 5 minutes.

Add flour and cook, stirring, for 4–5 minutes.

Gradually add white wine, stirring, and cook for 5 minutes.

Add stock, bay leaf and tomato paste and bring to a boil.

Reduce heat, discard bay leaf, and let simmer for 20 minutes.

Purée in batches in food processor or blender until smooth.

Return to low heat.

Stir in cream.

Discard bay leaf and add salt and pepper to taste.

Mussel Beach

Frankie and Annette never had it so good.

> 1 leek, thinly sliced
> 1 red pepper, seeded and thinly sliced
> 2 tsp minced garlic
> 1 tbsp butter
> ½ lb fresh mussels
> 3 cups fish stock or water
> 2 cups white wine

Brown leeks, red peppers and garlic in butter.

Wash mussels in cold water. Throw away any with shells that aren't tightly closed.

Add mussels to soup pot. Add stock and wine and bring to boil.

Reduce heat. Discard any mussels that aren't open.

Serve with fish-shaped Fancy Bread (see page 4).

White Clam Chowder

New England's claim to fame.

4 strips bacon, chopped
1 medium onion, diced
2 red peppers, seeded and diced
5 tbsp butter
5 tbsp flour
3 cans (5 oz each) clams
3 medium potatoes, peeled and cubed
1 cup white wine
1 oz brandy
3 cups clam juice, fish stock or water
2 cups 35 percent cream
Salt and black pepper

Cook bacon, onion and peppers in butter over medium heat until soft.

Add flour and cook, stirring, for 5 minutes.

Toss in clams and potatoes.

Gradually add wine, stirring; add brandy.

Add clam juice and bring to boil.

Reduce heat and simmer for 20 minutes.

Stir in cream and simmer for 10 minutes.

Add salt and pepper to taste.

Red Clam Chowder

Manhattan is home to this delicious delight.

>1 medium onion
>2 medium carrots
>3 medium potatoes, peeled
>1 tbsp butter
>3 cans (5 oz each) clams
>3 cups Clamato juice
>1 can (28 oz) plum tomatoes, drained
>   and tomatoes squished
>Zest of 1 orange

Dice onion, carrots and potatoes.

Cook in butter over medium heat for 5 minutes.

Add remaining ingredients and bring to a boil.

Reduce heat and simmer for 30 minutes.

Captain Jack's Fish Stew

A soup fit to celebrate a welcome home from the sea.

> 1 medium onion, chopped
> 1 medium carrot, diced
> 2 medium potatoes, peeled and diced
> 2 tsp minced garlic
> 1 tbsp butter
> 1 can (5 oz) clams, drained
> 1 can (4 oz) shrimp, drained
> 1 lb any white-fleshed fish, cubed
> 1 can (28 oz) plum tomatoes, undrained
>   and tomatoes squished
> 5 cups fish stock
> ¼ tsp fennel seeds
> ½ tsp saffron
> 1 bay leaf

Cook vegetables and garlic in butter over medium heat for 5 minutes.

Add remaining ingredients.

Bring to boil. Reduce heat and simmer for 20 minutes.

Discard bay leaf.

Serve with Garlic Croutons (see page 3).

Fish Soup with Potato Dumplings

It's like thunder and lightning: this soup's so good that it's frightening.

>2 medium carrots
>2 medium potatoes, peeled
>1 leek (white part only)
>2 lb any white-fleshed fish
>2 tbsp butter
>3 cups fish stock
>1 cup white wine
>1 bay leaf
>2 cups 35 percent cream
>Salt and black pepper
>30 Potato Dumplings (see page 6)

Cube carrots and potatoes and slice leek.

Cut fish into 1-inch cubes.

Cook vegetables and fish in butter over medium heat for 5 minutes.

Add stock, wine and bay leaf and bring to boil.

Reduce heat and simmer for 20 minutes.

Stir in cream and bring back to simmer.

Discard bay leaf and add salt and pepper to taste.

Poach dumplings in soup for 10 minutes.

Cup of Crab Soup

Bet you will have a bowl!

> ½ lb cooked ham
> 2 medium potatoes, peeled
> 1 lb imitation crab meat
> 2 tbsp butter
> 1 can (28 oz) plum tomatoes, undrained
>   and tomatoes squished
> 4 cups fish or chicken stock
> 2 cups 35 percent cream
> Salt and black pepper
> 2 cups grated cheddar cheese

Cube ham, crab and potatoes.

Cook ham, potatoes and crab in butter over medium heat for 5 minutes.

Add tomatoes and stock and bring to a boil.

Reduce heat and simmer for 20 minutes.

Stir in cream and simmer for an additional 5 minutes.

Add salt and pepper to taste.

Top with grated cheese and serve with Cheese Twisties (see page 2).

Leek and Stilton Soup

An elegant favourite made easy.

> 5 cups chopped leeks (white parts only)
> ½ cup butter
> 3 oz brandy
> 6 medium potatoes, peeled and chopped
> 5 cups chicken stock or water, cold
> 2 cups 35 percent cream
> ½ lb Stilton cheese (or substitute any blue cheese)
> Salt and black pepper

Cook leeks in butter until soft.

Add brandy and let cook for 1 minute.

Stir in potatoes. Add stock and bring to a boil.

Reduce heat and simmer for 20 minutes or until potatoes are soft.

Stir in cream and simmer for 10 minutes.

Crumble cheese and add to soup.

Add salt and pepper to taste.

Rosy Cheddar Soup

This cheery soup is so easy you'll be surprised how good it is.

> 2 cans (28 oz each) plum tomatoes,
>   undrained and tomatoes squished
> 2 cups chicken or vegetable stock
> 2 cups 35 percent cream
> Salt and black pepper
> 3 cups grated cheddar cheese

Bring tomatoes and stock to boil.

Reduce heat and simmer for 20 minutes.

Stir in cream and warm for 5 minutes.

Add salt and pepper to taste.

Stir in cheese just before serving.

Cream of Mushroom Soup

Beef stock and red wine make this version rich and flavourful.

> ¾ lb mushrooms, sliced
> 1 medium onion, diced
> 5 tbsp butter
> 5 tbsp flour
> 3 cups beef stock, cold
> 1 bay leaf
> 1 whole clove
> 1 cup red wine
> 2 cups 35 percent cream
> Salt and black pepper

Cook mushrooms and onions in butter until soft.

Add flour and cook, stirring, for 3–4 minutes.

Gradually add stock, stirring. Add bay leaf, clove and red wine and bring to boil.

Reduce heat and simmer for 20 minutes.

Stir in cream.

Discard bay leaf and clove and add salt and pepper to taste.

Cream of Asparagus Soup

Celebrate the arrival of spring with this salute to asparagus.

1 medium onion, diced
5 tbsp butter
5 tbsp flour
3 cups chicken stock, cold
2 cups 35 percent cream
1 cup white wine
4 cups asparagus tips
Pinch nutmeg
Salt and black pepper

Cook onion in butter until soft.

Add flour and cook, stirring, for 4–5 minutes.

Gradually add stock, stirring. Add cream and wine and bring to a boil.

Reduce heat to a simmer, add asparagus and nutmeg and cook for 15 20 minutes.

Purée in batches in a food processor or blender.

Add salt and pepper to taste.

Beer 'n' Cheese Soup

This soup is great with Garlic Croutons (see page 3).

> 1 medium onion, diced
> 5 tbsp butter
> 5 tbsp flour
> 2 cups chicken stock, cold
> 2 cups 35 percent cream
> 2 cups dark beer
> 1 bay leaf
> ¼ tsp ground allspice
> 12 oz white cheddar cheese, grated

Cook onion in butter until soft.

Add flour and cook, stirring, for 4–5 minutes.

Gradually add stock, stirring. Add cream, beer, bay leaf and allspice and bring to boil.

Reduce heat and simmer for 15 minutes.

Stir in cheese.

Discard bay leaf.

Raclette

This soup comes straight from the Swiss Alps to your kitchen.

⅓ medium onion, chopped
1 tsp minced garlic
4 medium potatoes, peeled and chopped
2 cups chopped mushrooms
1 tbsp olive oil
2 cups water
1 cup white wine
1 cup 35 percent cream
2 cups grated raclette or white cheddar cheese

Heat onions, garlic, potatoes and mushrooms in olive oil.

Add water and bring to boil.

Reduce to simmer and add wine.

Cook for 20 minutes.

Purée in batches in food processor or blender.

Return to low heat. Add cream and cheese.

Serve with Garlic Croutons (see page 3).

Tortellini Soup

Tortellini is a dumplinglike pasta usually stuffed with ricotta cheese or meat.

 1 leek (white part only), chopped
 1 tbsp butter
 6 cups chicken stock
 1-½ cups tortellini
 4 tbsp grated Parmesan cheese
 24 Meatballs (see page 5)

Brown leek in butter.

Add stock and bring to boil.

Add tortellini and cook for about 8 minutes or follow directions on package.

Reduce heat. Add Parmesan and cooked meatballs and simmer for 5 minutes.

Creamy Tortellini Soup

Pasta lovers will delight in this wonderful recipe.

> 5 tbsp flour
> 1 tsp minced garlic
> 1 leek (white part only), thinly sliced
> 5 tbsp butter
> 3 cups chicken stock, cold
> 3 cups homogenized milk
> 1-½ cups tortellini
> 1 cup grated mozzarella cheese
> 1 cup grated Parmesan cheese
> Salt and black pepper

Cook flour, garlic and leek in butter for 5 minutes, stirring constantly.

Gradually add stock, stirring; add milk.

Bring to boil and add tortellini. Cook for about 8 minutes or follow directions on package.

Reduce heat.

Add cheeses and salt and pepper to taste.

Hot Potato!

You won't be able to keep this soup around on a cool rainy day.

> 1 medium onion, diced
> 3 tsp minced garlic
> 1 tbsp curry powder
> 7 medium Yukon gold potatoes, peeled
>   and cut into large cubes
> 4 tbsp cooking oil
> 6 cups chicken or vegetable stock or water
> 2 bay leaves
> 1 tbsp dried thyme
> Salt and black pepper

Cook onion, garlic, curry powder and potatoes in oil, stirring, for at least 10 minutes. (The browner your potatoes and onions, the richer the flavour.)

Cover with stock, add bay leaves and bring to a boil.

Reduce heat and add thyme. Let simmer for 30 minutes or until potatoes are soft.

Discard bay leaves and purée soup in batches in a food processor or blender until smooth.

Add salt and pepper to taste.

Kissin' Cousins

Try this soup and see how well these two root vegetables get along.

2 medium sweet potatoes
1 acorn squash
2 medium potatoes
3 apples
6 cups chicken or vegetable stock or water
Salt and black pepper

Peel the vegetables and apples and cut into large pieces.

Add stock and bring to a boil.

Reduce heat and let simmer for 30 minutes or until vegetables are soft.

Purée in batches in food processor or blender until smooth.

Add salt and pepper to taste.

Carrot and Apple Soup

Thin slices of apple can be floated on top for a lovely garnish.

> 5 medium carrots
> 2 medium potatoes, peeled
> 2 ribs celery
> 3 apples
> 6 cups chicken or vegetable stock or water
> 1 cinnamon stick
> 1 bay leaf
> Pinch nutmeg
> Salt and black pepper

Peel and cut the vegetables and apples into large pieces.

Add stock and bring to boil.

Reduce heat and add cinnamon stick, bay leaf and nutmeg.

Let simmer for 30 minutes or until all vegetables are soft.

Remove bay leaf and cinnamon stick and purée in batches in food processor or blender until smooth.

Add salt and pepper to taste.

Blushing Cauliflower Soup

You might blush with the compliments this soup brings.

> 1 medium onion
> 2 medium parsnips
> 1 medium potato, peeled
> 1 head cauliflower
> 2 cups chicken or vegetable stock
> 1 can (28 oz) plum tomatoes, undrained
>   and tomatoes squished
> 3 cups homogenized milk
> ¼ tsp nutmeg

Peel and cut vegetables into large pieces. Reserve some cauliflower florets for garnish.

Put vegetables in soup pot, add stock and tomatoes and bring to boil.

Reduce heat, add milk and nutmeg, and let simmer for 30 minutes or until vegetables are soft.

Reduce heat and simmer for 30 minutes.

Purée in batches in food processor or blender until smooth.

Roasted Red Pepper Soup

When roasted, red peppers make a sweet and succulent soup.

> 6 large red peppers
> 2 tsp minced garlic
> 5 cups chicken or vegetable stock
> 2 cups 35 percent cream
> Salt and black pepper
> ½ lb feta cheese

Preheat oven or broiler.

Roast peppers on a baking tray in oven for 30 minutes or until the outside is brown and blistered.

Remove peppers, place them in a stainless steel bowl and cover with plastic wrap.

Let sit until cool.

Peel peppers and remove seeds.

Purée pulp in food processor or blender.

Combine peppers, garlic and stock in a soup pot and bring to a boil.

Reduce heat and let simmer for 10 minutes.

Stir in cream and simmer for 10 more minutes.

Add salt and pepper to taste.

Serve with crumbled feta cheese on top.

Twenty-Four Carat Soup

This one's a real gem.

> 6 medium carrots
> 2 medium potatoes, peeled
> 1 cup orange juice
> 4 cups chicken or vegetable stock
> 1 bay leaf
> ½ tsp ground ginger
> 1 cup 35 percent cream
> Salt and black pepper

Peel and cut vegetables into large pieces.

Combine first six ingredients and bring to boil.

Reduce heat and let simmer for 30 minutes.

Discard bay leaf and purée soup in batches in food processor or blender.

Return soup to low heat.

Add cream and salt and pepper to taste.

Serve with Cheese Twisties (see page 2).

Spinach and Mushroom Soup

Popeye got his strength from eating his spinach; he would love this powerful soup.

> 1 medium onion, sliced
> 1 tbsp minced garlic
> 3 cups sliced mushrooms
> 2 tbsp butter
> 1 cup apple juice
> 5 cups chicken or vegetable stock or water
> 1 bag (10 oz) spinach
> Salt and black pepper
> Parmesan cheese

Brown onions, garlic and mushrooms in butter.

Add apple juice and stock.

Bring to a boil. Reduce heat and let simmer for 5 minutes.

Remove and discard stems from spinach; chop leaves into large pieces.

Add to soup and cook for 10 minutes.

Add salt and pepper to taste.

Sprinkle with Parmesan cheese before serving.

Sweet and Sour Red Cabbage Soup

A dollop of sour cream can add a nice finishing touch to this hearty soup.

> 4 slices bacon, diced
> 1 medium red onion, chopped
> 4 cups shredded red cabbage
> ½ cup red wine vinegar
> 3 tbsp brown sugar
> ¼ tsp ground allspice
> 1 can (28 oz) plum tomatoes, undrained
>   and tomatoes squished
> 5 cups chicken stock
> Salt and black pepper

Brown bacon and onion on medium-high heat.

Stir in cabbage and vinegar and cook until soft.

Add sugar, allspice, tomatoes and stock and bring to a boil.

Reduce heat and simmer for 20 minutes.

Add salt and pepper to taste.

Watercress Soup

Serve with Garlic Croutons or Fancy Bread (see pages 3 and 4).

>1 medium onion, chopped
>2 tsp minced garlic
>3 bunches watercress, chopped
>2 tbsp butter
>4 cups chicken or vegetable stock
>2 cups 35 percent cream
>Salt and black pepper

Cook onions, garlic and watercress in butter over medium heat for 5 minutes.

Add stock and bring to boil.

Reduce heat and simmer for 15 minutes.

Purée in batches in food processor or blender.

Return to low heat and add cream.

Add salt and pepper to taste.

Sue's Green Pea Soup

This soup is as comforting as a kiss from Mom.

> 1 medium onion
> 2 ribs celery
> 2 medium potatoes, peeled
> 2 tbsp butter
> 4 cups chicken or vegetable stock
> 4 cups frozen peas
> 2 cups 35 percent cream
> Salt and black pepper

Cube onion, celery and potatoes.

Cook in butter over medium heat for 5 minutes.

Add stock and bring to boil.

Reduce heat and add peas. Let simmer for 20 minutes.

Purée in batches in food processor or blender.

Return to low heat and stir in cream.

Add salt and pepper to taste.

Roasted Eggplant Soup

A Mediterranean delight.

> 2 medium eggplants
> 1 medium onion, chopped
> 2 tsp minced garlic
> 4 zucchini, sliced
> 2 tbsp olive oil
> 1 can (28 oz) plum tomatoes, undrained
>   and tomatoes squished
> 4 cups chicken or vegetable stock
> Salt and black pepper

Preheat oven to 400°F.

Make slices in eggplant to allow steam to escape. Roast whole in the oven for 30 minutes or until pulp is soft.

Spoon pulp out of eggplants. Discard skin and chop pulp.

Cook onion, garlic and zucchini in oil over medium heat for 5 minutes.

Stir in eggplant and cook for 5 minutes.

Add tomatoes and stock and bring to boil.

Reduce heat and simmer for 15 minutes.

Add salt and pepper to taste.

Serve with Cheese Twisties (see page 2) or Garlic Croutons (see page 3).

Lisa's Vegetarian Borscht

Lisa loves her borscht with dill and yogurt.

> 1 apple, peeled
> 6 beets, peeled
> ½ head red cabbage
> 1 medium potato, peeled
> 1 medium red onion
> ¼ tsp ground cumin
> 1 tbsp cooking oil
> 5 cups vegetable stock or water
> 1 tbsp dried dill
> Yogurt (optional)

Dice the apple and the vegetables.

Cook onions and cumin in oil over medium heat for 3–4 minutes.

Add remaining ingredients.

Bring to boil, reduce heat and simmer for 30 minutes.

Serve with a dollop of yogurt, if using.

Pasta and Bean Soup

This soup offers a little taste of Italy without the expense of a Roman holiday. Stir in a little pesto for added zest.

4 slices bacon, chopped
2 tsp minced garlic
1 tbsp Italian seasoning
1 rib celery, diced
1 can (19 oz) white kidney beans
1 can (28 oz) plum tomatoes, undrained
   and tomatoes squished
3 cups chicken stock
½ cup shell pasta
Salt and black pepper

Cook bacon, garlic, Italian seasoning and celery on medium heat for 5 minutes.

Rinse and drain beans and add along with tomatoes and chicken stock.

Simmer for 30 minutes.

Meanwhile, cook pasta in 2 quarts boiling, salted water until soft but firm to the bite.

Drain and add pasta to soup.

Add salt and pepper to taste.

Black-Eyed Pea Soup

A great starter to any meal.

> 1 lb dried black-eyed peas
> 1 pork hock
> 2 tsp cooking oil
> 2 medium onions, chopped
> 1 medium carrot, chopped
> 6 cups water
> 2 bay leaves
> ¼ cup tomato paste
> Salt and black pepper

Soak peas overnight. (Remember to never salt peas or beans until after they're cooked.)

Brown pork hock in oil on medium-high heat.

Add onions and carrot and cook until soft.

Stir in peas.

Add water, bay leaves and tomato paste and bring to boil.

Reduce heat and let simmer for 1 hour or until peas are soft.

Discard bay leaves and add salt and pepper to taste.

Country Corn Chowder

An old favourite of the farmers around harvest time.

> 1 medium onion, diced
> 5 tbsp flour
> 5 tbsp butter
> 2 medium carrots
> 2 ribs celery
> 1 red pepper, seeded
> 4 medium potatoes, peeled
> 3 cups frozen corn
> 1 bay leaf
> 1 tsp dried thyme
> 6 cups milk

Cook onions and flour in butter over medium heat for 5 minutes.

Dice remaining fresh vegetables.

Add all vegetables and herbs to soup. Gradually add milk, stirring, and bring to boil.

Reduce heat and simmer for 15 minutes.

Italian Bread Soup

A treat for your taste buds and your budget, this soup provides a great way to use up day-old bread.

> 1 medium onion, chopped
> 3 tsp minced garlic
> 1 tbsp olive oil
> 2 cans (28 oz each) plum tomatoes,
>   undrained and tomatoes squished
> 3 cups chicken stock
> 8 slices day-old Italian bread

Cook onions and garlic in oil until soft.

Add tomatoes and stock.

Bring to boil. Reduce heat and simmer for 20 minutes.

Cut bread into large chunks and add to broth.

Simmer for 5 minutes and serve.

Lentil Soup

If you like your lentils spicy, try adding a pinch of cayenne.

> 1 medium onion, chopped
> 2 tsp minced garlic
> 2 tbsp cooking oil
> 4 cups water
> 1 can (28 oz) plum tomatoes, undrained
>   and tomatoes squished
> 1 can (13.5 oz) coconut milk
> 1 cup red lentils
> Salt and black pepper

Brown onions and garlic in oil.

Add water, tomatoes, coconut milk and lentils.

Bring to boil.

Simmer for 45 minutes.

Add salt and pepper to taste.

Tomato and Black Bean Soup

A taste from old Mexico—try this with a splash of hot sauce.

1 medium onion, chopped
3 tbsp minced garlic
1 tbsp cooking oil
1 tbsp butter
1 can (19 oz) black beans
1 can (28 oz) plum tomatoes, undrained
   and tomatoes squished
1 cup 35 percent cream
4 cups chicken stock or water
Salt and black pepper

Brown onions and garlic in oil and butter on medium heat.

Rinse and drain beans and toss them in along with the tomatoes.

Simmer for 30 minutes.

Add cream and stock and simmer for 5 minutes.

Add salt and pepper to taste.

Gary's Split Pea Soup

Our friend Gary cooks this one up during cool days on his boat. It soothes his skipper's heart.

2 slices bacon, diced
1 medium onion, diced
1 medium carrot, diced
1 rib celery, diced
1 tsp minced garlic
1 lb dried split peas
7 cups chicken stock
1 bay leaf
Salt and black pepper

Cook bacon, onion, carrot, celery and garlic over medium heat for 8 minutes.

Add peas, stock and bay leaf and bring to boil.

Reduce heat and let simmer for 1 hour or until peas are soft.

Discard bay leaf and add salt and pepper to taste.

Minty Mango Soup

More refreshing than a mint julep on a summer's day.

> 3 ripe mangoes
> 2 cups yogurt
> 4 cups apple juice
> 6 leaves fresh mint

Peel mangoes and clean the flesh away from the pit.

Purée the mango with the yogurt in a food processor or blender.

Add apple juice and pulse until the soup is smooth.

Chill for 2 hours and serve with fresh mint.

Plum and Buttermilk Soup

A sweet, smooth-as-velvet treat.

> 2 lb plums, peeled and pitted
> 3 cups water
> 2 tbsp brown sugar
> 2 tbsp lemon juice
> 2 cups buttermilk

Place plums (reserving a few slices for garnish), water, brown sugar and lemon juice in soup pot.

Bring to a boil. Reduce heat and simmer for 30 minutes.

Blend in batches in food processor or blender until smooth.

Return to low heat and whisk in buttermilk.

Let cool and garnish with thinly sliced plums.

Very Berry Soup

The excitement of spring in a bowl.

> 6 cups fresh or frozen berries
> 4 cups Cranraspberry juice
> 2 cups 35 percent cream
> 1 cup fruit-flavoured ice or sherbet
> ½ cup fresh berries, for garnish

Purée the 6 cups of berries with juice.

Whisk in cream.

Chill for 1 hour.

Serve with a dollop of fruit-flavoured ice and fresh berries.

Gazpacho

Olé! This cool soup will put a Spanish kick in your day.

2 green onions
½ medium red onion
1 red pepper, seeded
1 green pepper, seeded
1 cucumber, seeded
5 large ripe tomatoes
1 tsp minced garlic
1 chili pepper (optional)
5 cups V8 juice
2 tbsp olive oil
1 tsp salt
Black pepper

Slice green onions and cube the other vegetables.

Toss all ingredients in a large bowl, adding pepper to taste.

Purée in batches in food processor or blender. Avoid over-blending.